UNDOING ANXIETY
FULL SYSTEM RESTORE

New Science Reveals How to Break
the Cycles of Anxiety. A Powerful
Guide to Undo Anxiety.

WELCOME TO HAPPINESS

Introduction

New science reveals how to break the cycles of anxiety. Drawing from extensive research and personal experiences, author hassan kattan unveils a revolutionary approach to dealing with anxiety. Kattan introduces innovative techniques that redefine how we understand and address anxiety. His compassionate and insightful narrative gives readers a powerful guide to undo anxiety.

This book is the culmination of a decade of in-depth research conducted with individuals grappling with anxiety. A special thanks to all sufferers who contributed by sharing their personal experiences.

Undoing Anxiety: Full System Restore. A powerful guide to undo anxiety.

HASSAN KATTAN

(@MindBliss_)

Contents

What Causes Anxiety? — 8

How Does Pathogenic Bacteria Cause Anxiety? — 10

Undoing Anxiety — 12

- Step 1: Get Tested — 13
- Step 2: Doctor Prescription — 15
- Step 3: Retest to Verify Irradiation — 18
- Step 4: Eliminate the Residual Toxins from your System — 20

Welcome to Happiness — 25

Appendix: Affirmations — 27

DISCLAIMER: This guide is for informational purposes.

So What Causes Anxiety?

The primary cause of anxiety is **pathogenic bacteria** in the small intestines.

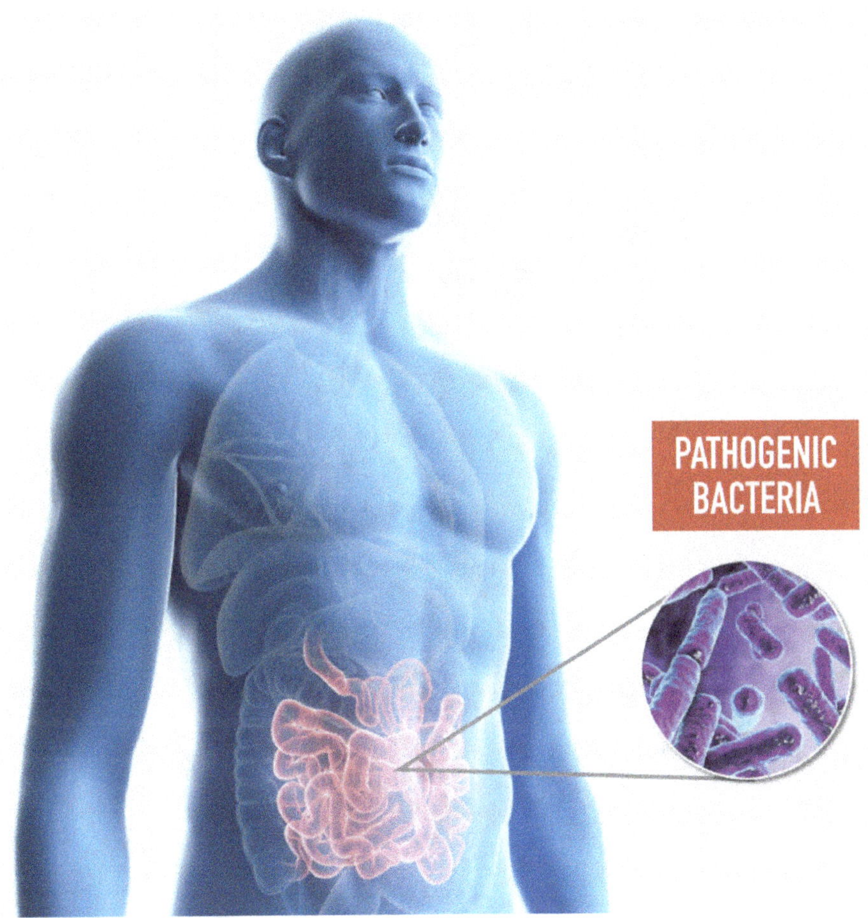

How does Pathogenic Bacteria Cause Anxiety?

Pathogenic bacteria release toxins inside the body, these toxins find their way to the brain triggering anxiety. Moreover, pathogenic bacteria adhere to the cells of your small intestines, creating a malevolent grip that induces a sensation of tension and heaviness in your head. It's akin to someone tying up your brain and tightening the tension.

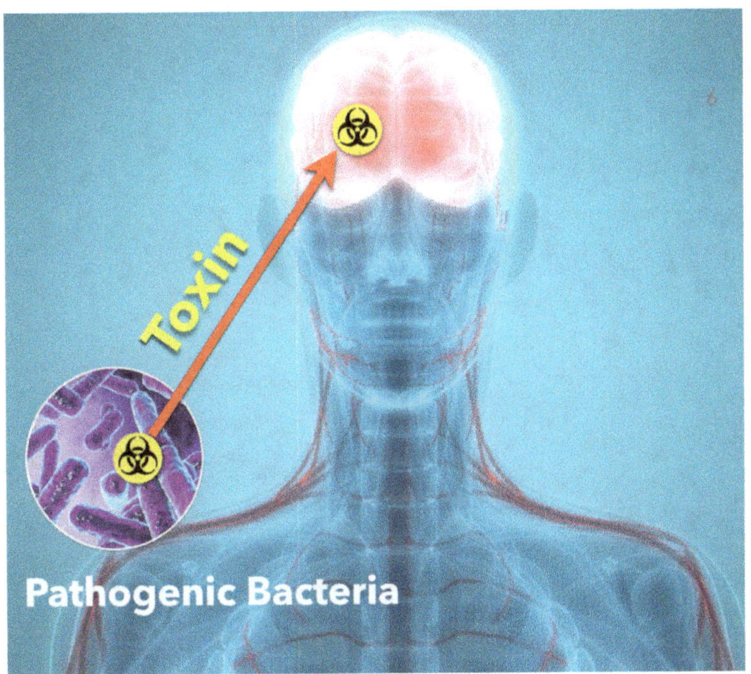

UNDOING ANXIETY

STEP 1

Get Tested

The purpose of getting tested is to identify the name of the pathogenic microbes present in the intestine, and the most effective method for this is through a **stool test**.

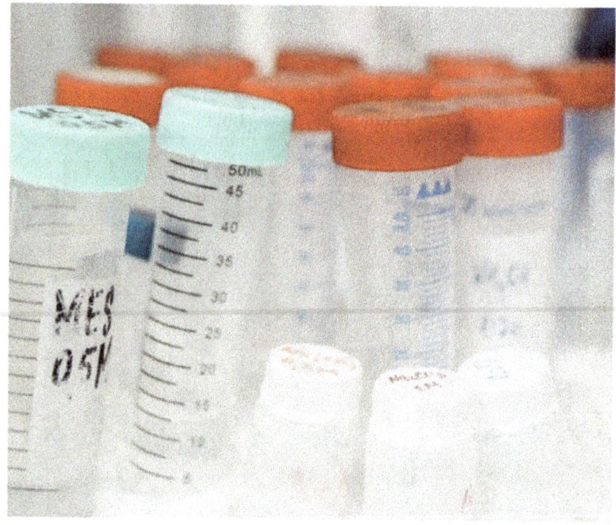

There are 3 stool tests for this purpose (stool is feces, caca):

1. **H. Pylori Stool Test:**
- Helicobacter Pylori is a pathogenic bacterium responsible for anxiety, panic attacks, OCD, depression, agoraphobia, rejection attacks, mood disorders and IBS.

2. **Bacterial Culture Stool Test:**
- Shows both pathogenic and beneficial bacteria
- The lab must conduct an Antimicrobial Susceptibility Test on the identified microbes.
- PCR tests are the most advanced & accurate
- Do not solely depend on the lab's determination of whether a bacterium is pathogenic; it may be inaccurate. Consult a doctor for a more reliable assessment.
- An example of pathogenic bacteria: *Alpha Haemolytic Streptococcus* is responsible for crippling germophobia, phobias, phobia attacks, anxiety, panic attacks, OCD, depression, rejection attacks, mood disorders, joint pain (neck), and IBS.

3. **Parasite Stool Test:**
- Collected over 3 days

STEP 2

Doctor Prescription

When pathogenic bacteria or microbes are detected in your stool test, your doctor can utilize the lab's antimicrobial susceptibility test results to identify an effective treatment for eradicating the pathogens. This test involves the lab conducting analyses to determine which antimicrobial medication will successfully eliminate the identified pathogenic microbes.

An example of pathogenic bacteria: *Alpha Haemolytic Streptococcus*

STEP 3

Verifying Eradication

Repeat the test(s) two months post-treatment to confirm eradication of the pathogenic bacteria or microbe.

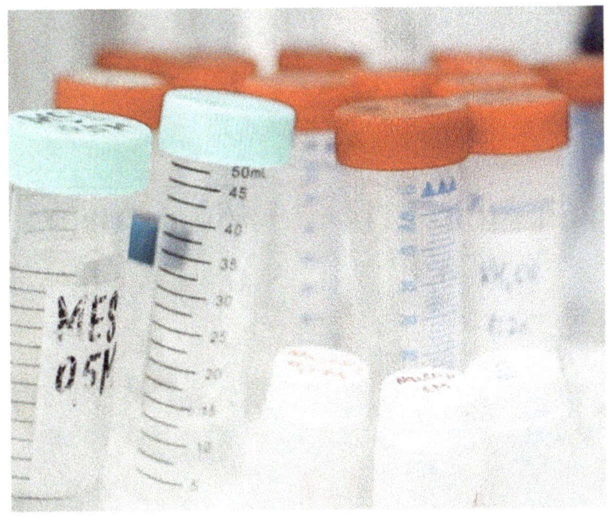

STEP 4

Eliminate the Residual Toxins

Even after eliminating the pathogenic bacteria, toxins persist in your system. To restore your body and counteract the inflicted disorders, it's crucial to eliminate these residual toxins.

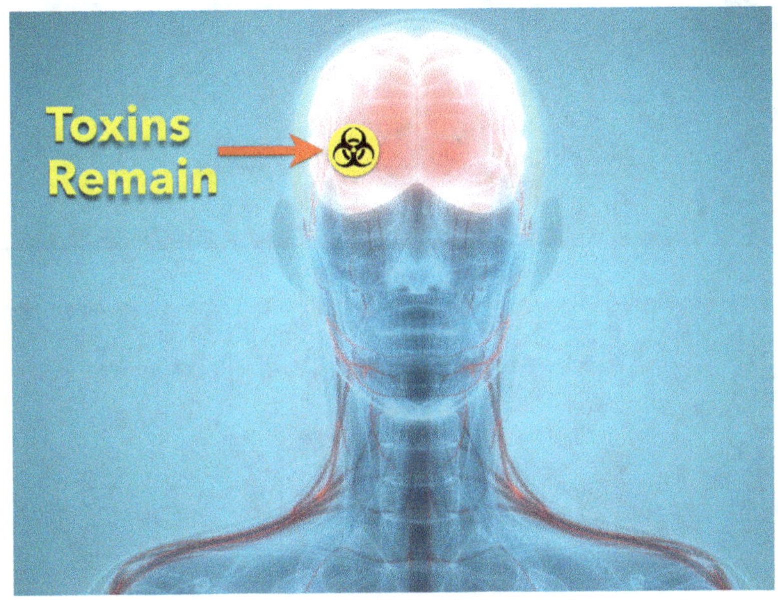

In order to eliminate the residual toxins, you will need three things:

FRESH GINGER: Disables the residual toxins for 1 hour

MEDJOOL DATES: Eliminates some residual toxins from your system

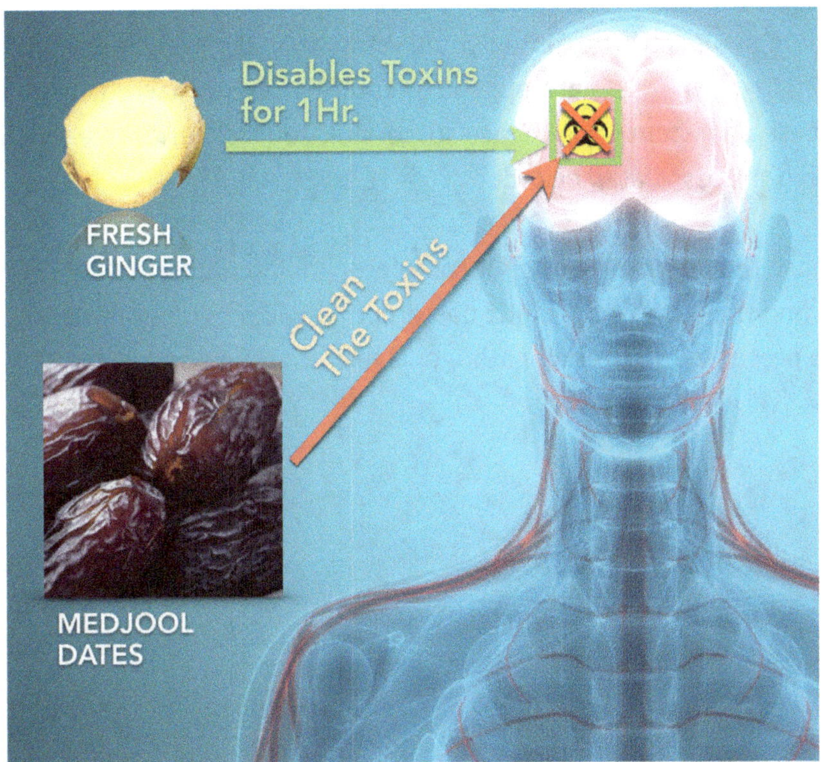

Currently, there are lingering toxins in your system that cannot be eliminated with dates or ginger. In this final step, you'll require probiotic bacteria capable of overriding these persistent toxins. Once successful, you'll experience a sense of liberation from the associated disorders.

If you still sense that your recovery is incomplete, it might indicate either: The necessity to find the suitable probiotic bacteria that will override the lasting toxins **or** the presence of lingering pathogenic microbes in your gut.

Welcome to Happiness

APPENDIX

AFFIRMATIONS

You are
worthy of
love and
respect.

You are safe.

You are a reservoir of
untapped potential.

Breathe
deeply, you
are here
and now.

Cherish the
moment.

You are capable
of overcoming
any challenges
that come your
way.

Rainbows
follow even
the heaviest
storms.

Let go of fear
and worry,
welcome peace
into your heart.

Every step
counts.

Believe in yourself.

Your uniqueness
is a gift to the
world.

You are worthy
of peace and
happiness.

Never give up..

Keep moving
forward.

You embrace
each moment
with gratitude.

Every challenge is
an opportunity for
growth and
learning.

You are resilient,
setbacks are
stepping stones
to your triumph.

Your journey
is unique and
filled with
endless
possibilities.

Embracing
change
empowers
you to evolve
and thrive.

Your potential
is limitless.

You choose
peace over
worry.

You welcome
positive
change with
open arms.

Each step
you take
is a step
towards
growth.

You matter.

You are
beautiful

Your mind
is calm,
and your
body is
relaxed.

Each breath
you take fills
you with
calm and
tranquility.

You are
surrounded
by love and
support.

Success is a
natural
outcome of
your efforts.

You are grateful
for the abundance
in your life.

You believe in
your abilities.

You face
challenges
with grace
and
resilience.

Your
potential is
limitless.

You welcome
positive
change with
open arms.

You are
confident
and capable.

You are a
beacon of love
and kindness.

You are a
magnet for
success and
prosperity.

Today, you choose happiness.

You radiate
positivity
and joy.

You are deserving
of success and
happiness.

You are resilient
and strong.

You're
stronger than
you think.

Shine your
light.

Your journey matters.

Today is a
new chance.

You are
serene and
peaceful.

Visualize
tranquility and
peace your
mind.

Love yourself

Breath in for
four seconds,
breathe out for
four seconds.

Abundance flows
effortlessly into
your life.

You've overcome
challenges before and
can do it again.

Trust in your
ability to navigate
whatever comes
your way.

Breathe in
calmness, exhale
tension

You are in control,
and you choose
positivity

Trust in your
ability to handle
whatever the
future holds.

Radiate
positivity in
every step.

Positivity and
abundance flow
through you.

You embrace
each moment
with gratitude.

You are
wealthy.

You are
successful.

You are energetic
and powerful.

You attract
good
things into
your life.

Be proud of
yourself for what
you achieved
endured.

I choose
peace over
worry.

You cultivate
inner peace
and harmony.

You are
constantly
evolving and
growing.

You find joy in
the simplest
moments.

You attract
abundance
into your
life.

You are capable
of achieving great
things.

Success is not just
a destination; it's
your journey.

Success
effortlessly
gravitates
towards you.

Your journey
is unique and
worthwhile.

Your presence is a
gift to the world,
and you make a
positive impact
wherever you go.

Challenges are
opportunities for
you to showcase
your strengths &
resilience.

You are surrounded
by positive energy
and attract good
things.

Positive thoughts
attract positive
outcomes.

Resilience
is your
greatest
asset.

Happiness and
success are
within your
reach.

Embrace
each day
with
optimism.

You are resilient
and strong.

Your efforts pave
the way for a
brighter future.

Your
potential
knows no
bounds.

Your are capable
of achieving your
dreams.

Your mindset
determines your
success, and you
choose positivity.

In stillness, find
your inner
strength.

Navigate life
with courage
and grace.

Your efforts today pave the way for a brighter tomorrow.

Embrace each
day with a
positive mindset.

You have the
strength to face
whatever comes
your way.

Every challenge
is an opportunity
for growth.

Your potential
is limitless.

Your resilience
is your greatest
asset.

You are
capable.

You deserve
happiness.

Illuminate the
world with your
authentic self.